My Life in Black and White
A book of experiences

Kori D. Miller

My Life in Black and White: A Book
of Experiences

Published by
Back Porch Writer Press

Fremont, NE 68025
www.backporchwriter.com

Printed in the United States of
America

Edited by Larry Miller

ISBN 978-0-9914756-1-2
Second Edition

Contents

Blue Ribbons and Tomato Soup

When I was in college, I took a composition course. The professor had us writing about all types of topics. By that time, I was comfortable with my racial identity. When asked, I would initially respond "human." When I would get the "deer in the headlight look" in return, I'd explain that I'm interracial.

One of our assignments was to write a poem. Race was on my mind a lot. I don't remember why. At any rate, the poem I created focused on the numerous differences between people. In the end, though, I simply said we all have red blood and blue veins.

"Blue Ribbons and Tomato Soup" probably took me less than an hour to compose. It got tucked away into a bin somewhere and forgotten, but the title and sentiment has stayed with me.

I hope it stays with you. We are more alike than we are different. Find the similarities.

KDM

Fremont, NE

For my parents and husband, who always have encouraged me to pursue my goals, and my children, who are a constant source of hope, laughter and writing material.

And, for my friends who saw me through a few dark days. Thank you. - KDM

Grade School Lessons

"There are no college courses to build up self-esteem or high school or elementary school. If you don't get those values at a early age, nurtured in your home, you don't get them."

T. D. Jakes

First Crush

My first crush was a boy named James. He had blondish hair and glasses. It was 1st grade. That crush lasted until the 8th grade and survived a change in schools. I don't know what it was about him. He was simply the nicest boy I knew at the time.

When my parents placed me in a Catholic School for 1st grade, it took a lot of adjusting on my part. I came from a Montessori school. I did not understand the nuns and their strange rules. My 1st grade teacher assigned James to be my "buddy." From that day on I was smitten. I still can recall him guiding me to my new seat in the classroom.

It was no secret how I felt about James. All of our school pals knew and teased us. His face turned several shades of red, but I remember how nice he always was. He never made fun of me for liking him. The fact that he is white never crossed my mind. The fact that I'm not white never crossed his. Back then, no one cared. We were more caught up in the "oh, he has cooties" stage. We were simply friends. It's sad when you realize those days are gone.

I don't know what happened to James. I could probably find out in this day of Facebook and Twitter, but I don't know if I really want to know. Maybe, just maybe, preserving the memory of something so innocent and simple is a good thing.

Black Cats and Black-Clad Heroes

When I was in 1st or 2nd grade, one of our assignments was to color a picture of a cat. I don't recall if it happened to be close to Halloween. I colored my cat, handed it in and was very proud of it. Then, one fateful day, Sister Something or Other decided to share everyone's pictures.

She held up picture after picture saying, "Oh, look at the colors in this one!" and, "So and so stayed in the lines."

Then, I saw my picture. I don't remember exactly what she said. What I do remember is this: She held my picture up as an example of something ugly. I colored the entire cat black. I even stayed in the lines (something I rarely do as an adult!)

I love black cats. For years I thought, "If I have a black cat, I'll name it Sheik." To me, the most beautiful animals are black. I love panthers (even though they actually

10

have stripes or spots), domestic black cats and dogs, wolves, etc. If it's black, I'll probably like it. I really don't know why. Maybe it's because I associate black with a sense of mystery. I don't recall a time in my life when I thought of the color black as bad, ugly or evil.

Here is an interesting note: When I think about heroes created by our American culture, there are very few instances when the hero actually wore black, but when they did, I loved them! I adored Zorro, with his precise blade. Hop-A-Long Cassidy also was a favorite. Then, of course, there are Batman and Cat Woman. But, and this is a big but, when I was coming up, there were very few heroes who wore black.

I don't know why Sister Something or Other did what she did. Maybe she didn't like black because she had to wear it every day. Nevertheless, my heroes wore black.

Old School Play Dates

When I was just turning 8 years old, my family moved to a new neighborhood. In the beginning I believed the boulevard on which we lived didn't have many, if any black people. This was very different from our previous neighborhood where there was a mix of white, Hispanic, and black kids. From my perspective, my brother and I were all alone. It was not unusual for us to be the only nonwhite kids or one of maybe five in our classes. As we got to know our new neighborhood, I learned that we weren't completely alone.

Around the corner on Mary Street, there were two Mexican families with whom we shared countless hours of hide and seek, kick the can and mini-campouts. White and black friends from near and far (okay, maybe five blocks away) also would join in the fun. We would play until we heard our parent's call ... 'cause you know we ignored all time-keeping devices! Our play area extended through at least three yards. During spring and summer, when the light extended the night, we'd spend hours outside.

Those truly were The Days. I have very fond memories of staying up talking in a tent we pitched in the Gonzales' yard, playing charades and Truth or Dare. This was "back in the day" when brothers and sisters hung together like glue. Not just because we had to, but because we wanted to. We had a great time.

Now, I struggle with ways to expose my children to other children. We live in the country where there aren't families with youngsters right next door. Less than a mile away a registered sex offender hangs his hat. We go to local parks in town where parents (mostly mothers, I must admit) worry if their kid throws rocks (at all) or play fights with another child. There doesn't seem to be room for kids to simply be kids. The notion that kids fight and the playground is the great equalizer seems to be lost on many these days.

I long for the days when my children will be able to run outside without worrying about some crazy person doing something truly stupid or some parent overreacting because some kid, any kid, threw some rocks on a frickin' playground. And I long for the days when "play date" actually means my children made some friends at a playground and said, "Hey! I'll see you tomorrow! Same place, same time. Be there or be square."

That would be utopia.

Bigots in Baptist Clothing

After my family moved to a new neighborhood that was not as integrated as the one we'd left, my brother and I transferred to a different school. We quickly made new friends in our Catholic school, and our neighborhood, where the majority of kids attended public school.

Since we attended a Catholic school, our primary exposure to church originated from this experience. Many of my public-school friends attended Baptist or Lutheran churches. I didn't decide to become Catholic until the 8th grade, but before and after that decision, I attended services with many friends at other Christian churches.

One of my earliest memories is of attending Baptist services with my friend, Cari. She was a year or so older than I. Her parents were pretty strict, which immediately

15

caused Cari to rebel. She spent a lot of time at my house, and as most kids did, called my parents mom and dad. Her parents, in contrast to mine, were professed bigots. They especially didn't like black people, and while they didn't like our friendship at first, they didn't stop it. In fact, they welcomed me to their church.

Now that I'm older, I wonder what motivated them to do that. Were they trying to save me? If so, from what? My primary memory of their church was the great food during social hour, after the service. That was the only reason for going, and it was the only aspect that made it more interesting than the Catholic church that I attended.

Cari's family wasn't unique in their openly hostile view of other races. I grew up with lots of friends whose parents and families were, and perhaps still are, bigots. They believed that if their child hung out with me, then their child would get into trouble.

My brother and I graduated from private high schools. We also graduated from college. My brother received his MBA while having a successful career. I worked 10 years and attained success in one career, then decided to open a business of my own. We've traveled extensively. We accomplished all of these things because we, for the most part, stayed out of trouble. He and I are very goal-oriented people. In our minds, accomplishing our goals is really just a matter of when, not if.

What happened to Cari and other friends like her? I don't really know. Many of those friendships faded as high school and college became more of my reality. Some did not finish high school due to pregnancy and drug usage. Others simply became stuck. I have to chuckle a bit when I think about all the rude, insensitive comments that were made by those parents. In all their efforts to keep their children

My life in black and white:

A book of experiences

from a perceived threat, the real threat was staring them in the mirror.

Hey, Nigger!

I don't remember having many challenges when we first moved into our new neighborhood. That all changed when a black family moved into a house up the block and behind ours. I was outside playing in the backyard when I heard a word I wasn't accustomed to hearing: "nigger." In fact, this was the first time I remember ever being called a nigger. It was really confusing. At this point in my life, I was black. I was not an interracial kid. I was a black kid. Why would they call me that?

The family had two girls and one boy. My newspaper route took me past their house every day. And just about every day, the oldest girl was on me. My best friend usually did the route with me. When she did, that girl left me alone. I don't know why.

I remember wishing that they'd move or that someone would be with me all the time when I walked the route. Then, one day he appeared out of nowhere. He was big and beautiful with amazing blue eyes. My dad called him Avatar. To me, he was a hero. He was a Siberian Husky. For two weeks he walked my route with me every day. He hung out on our front porch all day and night. It was obvious he belonged to someone. He knew basic commands. Then one day he vanished. It was like he knew I didn't need him anymore.

I don't remember what happened to that family. One day, they just didn't matter to me anymore. It might have been when I learned why the oldest girl hated me so much. A friend explained to me that the girl had a crush on a boy that happened to be a friend of mine. Not a close friend. He was a guy in the neighborhood. I liked him, but never really told him. We were young, but not so young that we didn't understand the rules. He is white. His family would never allow him to see a black girl, even one that was mixed. The other girl was jealous of my friendship with this boy. That was it. How petty.

Note: I'd like to add a little 40 plus year old insight here. In my experience, no healthy relationship involves jealousy. Sure, you might get upset for a minute that your friend is getting lots of attention, or that some guy is more interested in your friend than in you – That's normal. But, at the end of the day, you need to be comfortable in your own skin. You need to find your path, and work it. Friendships, boyfriends, and girlfriends move through your life as you figure yourself out. That's good. And, it's okay. All of your experiences, and how you react to them, create the person you'll become, so pay attention. Surround yourself with supportive people who believe in you.

My life in black and white:

A book of experiences

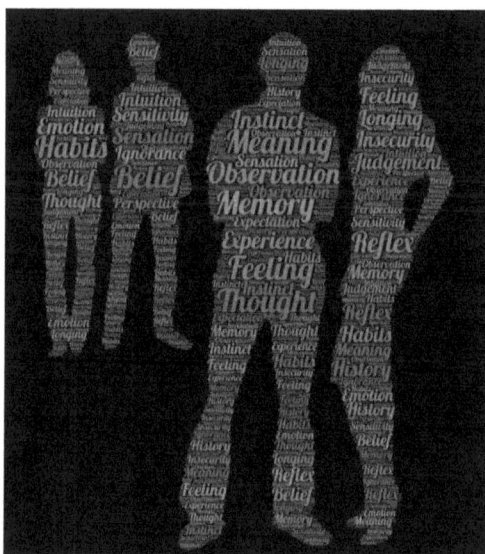

My life in black and white:

A book of experiences

High School and Other Horror Stories

"High school isn't a very important place. When you're going you think it's a big deal, but when it's over nobody really thinks it was great unless they're beered up." Stephen King, *Carrie*

Zebras, Half-breeds and Oreo Cookie

I was 12 years old when I realized I'm not black. That probably seems like a really strange thing to say, but it's true. Everyone experiences a time in life when something dramatic happens; a turning point. It's like that poem by Robert Frost that says, "two roads diverged in a wood and I, I took the one less traveled by and that has made all the difference." Though I didn't know it at the time, I was about to travel a road less traveled, and yes, it, I realize now, made all the difference.

When I was in the 7th grade I had a crush on a boy in my class. This boy was cute and popular. We were friends. At least, I thought we were. He is white and when he found out I had a crush on him everything changed. I became Kori, the zebra who sat in front of him in class. That year was the worst year of my life. Nearly every day I was greeted with a litany of names all focusing on the simple fact that my mother is white and my father is black.

Until the age of 12 my parents raised my brother and me as black children. Things were different now. I had to figure out who I was. If I could figure this one thing out, I could handle anything life threw my way.

The first serious boyfriend I had is white. I remember everything about him: the color of his hair, the color of his eyes, the way the corners of his mouth curled when he smiled. I remember how we met. Everything was perfect. Okay, not everything. This 16-year-old boy's parents threatened to kick him out of the house if he didn't stop seeing me. My father offered to take him in temporarily if this happened. That was when I learned concretely what my family is all about.

I grew up with parents who always took in "strays." If you

needed a home, our door was open. People crowded our house on all the holidays when there was nowhere else for them to go. All this from a couple of atheists. Go figure.

By the time I entered college I knew who I was. It didn't matter anymore what other people thought. As far as I was concerned, the world had to accept me on my terms. I learned that I had the best of both worlds if I made the choice. I learned accepting myself is a far greater thing than accepting others.

I would be lying if I said it was fun or easy all the time, but I also would be lying if I said the worst of these experiences wasn't worth all that I learned. I am married now. Someone asked me if I married a white man or a black man. I smiled and asked, "Are those my only choices?"

Note: This essay was originally published in *Fine Lines Literary Journal*, Summer 2007 edition. It was written for a college course during the late 80s or early 90s. I included it here, and in *Fine Lines*, without any major changes.

It was an interesting experience digging it out of a box, dusting it off, and reading it after so many years had passed. I can recall with amazing clarity how it felt to experience those things that I described. I'm not one for living in the past, but I understand that some experiences are important to share.

Because we all use Facebook now, I was able to get into touch with my former boyfriend. He provided more insights into the situation. His father was the reason we couldn't see each other. I always thought it was his mother. You know what they say about assumptions. Lesson learned.

The Color of Friendship

From the moment I saw his gorgeous color, dark hair and amazing smile, I was hooked. A group of friends and I were visiting Worlds of Fun in Kansas City, MO. Another girl and I decided not to get on a ride with everyone else. While we waited, we saw him. He was with a few friends. Somehow we struck up a conversation and invited them to hang out at our hotel, later. We thought it would be fun for all of us to get together.

Now, let me back up a bit. We were on a chaperoned trip. In our hotel, my other friends had already seen a group of white guys that they wanted to "get to know." This other girl and I thought nothing of inviting a few more guys to the party. We quickly discovered how wrong we were.

Our friends felt uncomfortable around the Middle-Eastern guys we met. To this day, I don't know why.

What I remember was that it was okay for them to invite strange white guys to our room, but not for us to invite strange foreign guys to our room. My friend and I spent a few hours chatting with the guys outside.

This incident caused a large rift in my friendship with this group. These girls had been my friends since freshman year. We were known as "the rat pack." After returning to the room, they proceeded to tell me everything that was wrong about what I did, everything they didn't like about me, and how bad an influence I was on the other girl. By the end of the discussion I knew exactly where I stood with each one of them. Senior year was going to be a very different experience.

Before classes resumed, I had a few conversations with one or two of them. It was understood that I no longer was welcome in the group. We would be cordial to each other. I don't recall any problems with any of them. I hung with other people. I always knew a lot of people, so losing what was considered my "core" group didn't matter to me. What mattered was finally knowing what they thought of me, and learning that they were never my friends.

I told my parents everything about the incident. My mother took me back to Kansas City to see Ali. And when Ali drove to Omaha just to see me for a few hours, my parents were impressed. He and I corresponded for a while, but after he relocated to California our communication naturally fell off. The experience had run its course. Something I think my parents foresaw, which in retrospect, is probably why they were okay with me seeing him.

I've had very few female friends over the years. It seems that when I allow too many into my life, I get disappointed. The ones I do have, I trust. I know that each one will have my back if the need arises. We are simply "there" for each other, without question. We pick up where we are. We laugh, cry, and say good-bye until next time. That is the true color of friendship.

Note: Friendships aren't always easy. It's more difficult to form friendships as you move into adulthood and start a family. At least, that's true for me. I'm an introvert, and a bit shy. So, if you're like me, then work a little harder to form those lasting friendships, now. They'll be there for you later.

A White Boy in Dark Skin

When I was 16 or 17, I met a guy who was afraid of black people. Specifically, he was afraid of black men. Had he been 100 per cent white, I might have understood -- a little. This particular guy, and his younger brother, are interracial. So, why was he afraid of black men?

Once, we were strolling along Gene Leahy Mall in Omaha, NE. As a group of five or six young black guys approached us, my friend became increasingly nervous. I asked what was wrong. He couldn't explain. I kept telling him everything would be okay, but what he desperately wanted to do was turn around and go in the other direction. He needed to get away from them. It was the strangest experience. He didn't know them. This boy had not met my father or brother yet, so I was concerned how that would go.

Our relationship didn't last long.

I couldn't continue seeing someone who, from my perspective, was weak. And, I couldn't get my head around the fact that he was afraid of his own people. I blamed his parents, whom, admittedly, I never met. They are white. They adopted this young man and his brother. I thought that was great, except that they appeared to be teaching them to fear black people and only trust white people. My opinion was based on numerous conversations with him.

I always thought his situation was sad. It's difficult walking the line between two seemingly opposed races. For me, having both my parents always available to field questions and hear my frustrations was critical to my evolving into a strong person not afraid to buck the system, walk that line and say, "I'm interracial. Deal with it!" I often wonder what happened to that guy.

His being adopted by a white couple wasn't the issue. His being adopted by a white couple who, from what I understood, wasn't teaching him about his background or culture, was an issue.

A child begins to learn who he is, that is to say, form an identity, based on who his family is, and how that family interacts with him or her. If a child is afraid of black people, for instance, it's the parent's fault. Children aren't born afraid of anything except falling and loud noises. Everything else is learned behavior.

So, I couldn't understand this young man, and at the time, I perceived him to be a weak person. Unfair, perhaps, but I was young. Now, I'm simply curious about the person he became.

Oui! Oui! No, I'm Not French!

You know you're living in a city filled with bigots when it's okay for you to be a French black person but not an American black person, and you live in the United States!

When I was 16, I briefly dated a white guy whose parents believed I was from France. This is what the boy told them so that he could date me. It was a good thing I'd learned some French growing up and was studying it in school. If not, I would have failed the little tests they gave me, periodically.

Here's an interesting observation: I come from a middle-class family. I attended private schools until college. This young man came from a working-class family and attended public schools. He never even attended college. College wasn't important to his family. Isms are interesting. The fact that we came from different economic classes, and mine was higher, didn't bother them, but the mere thought of their son dating a half-black person was unthinkable, unless I came from another country.

Our courtship, and I use that term loosely, didn't last long. I was getting older and more confident. Wasting time dating people who had "that problem" was quickly loosing appeal. I'd already fallen hard for another white guy whose family had "that problem," and I was in recovery mode. So, I moved on. We remained friends for a time and then went our separate ways.

I don't know, yet, how I'll handle this when my children are old enough to date. They'll, no doubt, encounter people like I did. My children can "pass." For those too young to understand what this means, I'll explain. My children look white in every way. People will discriminate against them because of me. I know we will have many long, and sometimes painful discussions about this as they get older. My only hope is that I handle their questions, concerns and fears as well as my mother and father did. Without the guidance and understanding of my parents, I wouldn't have weathered the storm that was my adolescence.

White Boys Don't Dance in Nebraska

When you attend a single-sex, predominately white high school, your dating pool immediately shrinks. Most, actually almost all of the boys I met were white. A few weren't, but there wasn't a single black young man that I met in my day-to-day environment. Not one. Dating in high school is challenging enough without adding the "I'm not completely white" component.

I could share so many stories I really don't know where to begin. One that I find humorous now, but didn't at the time, happened when friends and I went to a club called The Edge of Town.

I decided to ask a boy to dance. As usual, most of the boys in attendance were white. I said to a friend, "Watch this." I walked over to some boys pinned up against a wall. I asked the first to dance. He said, "no." I asked the next one. He said, "no." This went on until I reached the last boy, who also said, "no." I finally asked, "Why not? Don't you like to dance? Why are you here if you don't want to dance?" He didn't know what to say. I just walked away.

It wasn't the first time this happened, but I did get to a point where I didn't care. After numerous talks with "The Wise One," aka, my dad, I realized that there could have been a few explanations for the behavior of the boys I met during high school. Some may have been intimidated because I asked them out rather than wait for them to make a move. Others might not have liked me because I'm not completely white. Some might really have liked me, but not know how to approach me. Others might not have known how to dance! I like that last explanation. It seemed to hold true through college.

My life in black and white:

A book of experiences

College Days

"College is a refuge from hasty judgment." Robert Frost

Good Hair

I'm not sure where the notion of "good hair" came from, but it's an evil thing to say to any child. What's wrong with curly, kinky hair? There are white people trying to look like us while we struggle to look more like them. It's so true that people want what they can't have, but will try very hard to get it, even to the point of teaching children that they should reject how they see themselves.

In college, I began to realize just how ridiculous this all was. Some black students had challenges accepting me. I wasn't "black enough." I still don't know exactly what that means. According to some, I didn't date black men, I studied all the time, I thought I was white, I talked white, etc. Apparently all of that "evidence" meant I wasn't "black enough."

What I found so interesting was that the majority of my critics were females who straightened their hair. I was in the process of letting my hair grow again and decided against straightening it, something I had been doing since the age of 12. I couldn't respect those females. If they were so black, why did they reject their curls? I embraced my curls. Okay, on some days I still curse them, but I do embrace them. I can have long, curly hair or short, curly hair and I'm just as happy. Hell, I grew out my hair just so I could have a pony tail and NOT have to worry about my hair!

There is no such thing as "good hair." There is simply hair or no hair. I recall listening to Robin Roberts talk about her battle with cancer. She lost her hair, as many people with cancer do. She told herself, "I am not my hair." And, that is all there is to the debate. Good hair, bad hair, I am not my hair, and neither is anybody else.

Life as a Non-Mexican

One of the guys I dated in college is Mexican-American. We met after I attended a welcome function for nonwhite students at the cultural center on campus. He was very active in MASA, the Mexican-American Student Association while I was active in APU, African Peoples' Union.

On one occasion, I remember sitting in the culture center common area just before a MASA meeting began. A girl, whose name I don't recall, asked "Are you coming to the meeting?" I remember being surprised by the question. My response was, "Why would I? I'm not Mexican." She was taken aback. It was then that I realized most of his friends and acquaintances thought I was Mexican.

It wasn't the first time that happened and it definitely wasn't the last. On two separate occasions, once while traveling across the Mexican border with my parents, the other with friends, I was stopped by the border patrol. With my parents, the officer questioned where I was born. He didn't believe my answer, but who would lie and say they are from Nebraska? When I realized he didn't believe me, I pointed to my parents and said, "Black, white, brown, that's how that works." My father was a little upset that I didn't answer quickly, but I was shocked I was even stopped. Years later, upon returning from Tijuana with friends, I was the only one questioned by the border patrol. I laughed. I was in the car with two Mexicans and a white girl!

It happened so many times, and still does. Some Spanish speakers will even begin speaking to me in Spanish. Eeeck! I don't know much Spanish beyond counting to 10, basic greetings and asking for the time. My French background helps out a little. When I lived in Miami, I would say, "I should get a t-shirt that reads: "I know I look like I know Spanish, but I don't."

Men Are Like a Box of Chocolates

I recall my father saying once that he always hoped I'd marry a black man. I don't know why he felt this way; I never asked. What I do know is that there were none around me in high school, well not really. In college, I remember saying to my father, "Now, maybe I'll get to date black guys." What an utter and complete disappointment. Uh oh. There, I wrote that down. Go get offended.

What I observed in college was the mistreatment, and in some cases, abuse of my friends over and over again. There were exceptions. There were three guys I really liked, but they or I were never available at the same time. I dated one black guy from a different campus. What did he do? We agreed to split our phone bills since we were talking long distance. Did he ever pay? No. I'm not saying white guys are different; they aren't. I simply had higher

47

expectations for some reason.

I spent hours talking with my father about the black guys my friends dated and the ones I was meeting. He finally said: "Some men are just assholes." Well, that was true.

So, I never intentionally avoided black men. My policy was not to date assholes. A man from any race, ethnicity, or culture could be an asshole. If they were, then I wouldn't date them. A simple rule, really. One I found useful again and again. Oh, and don't date football players. That was my brother's rule, and he was a football player!

My dating pool was wide open because I opted to date men based on whether I liked them. I never regretted dating a guy because of his race or ethnicity. I learned a lot from the experiences. One of the best benefits was learning how to cook a variety of foods: Thai, Mexican, Korean, Chinese, Middle Eastern -- I love great food.

Men really are like a great box of chocolates. I'm thinking Callebaut chocolates here. Sometimes you get one that just isn't to your liking so you toss it out. Then, you find that one piece that makes your eyes close as the corners of your mouth begin to turn up. Yep, a good man is definitely like a great box of chocolates. You explore until you find just the right flavor.

Teachable Moments

Imagine this: You're with a group of school-age kids, 10-12 years old. All of them are white. They come from families where the "n" word gets thrown about like a ball. It's completely normal to them. Then, one day, those kids meet you, the YMCA counselor who isn't white.

My group talked to me about everything from race, to liking girls/boys, to sports. They knew I would listen and be honest with my answers. I challenged them when they made sweeping generalizations about other people. I encouraged them to seek out answers to their questions. I watched for teachable moments. One hot summer day I was presented with the best teachable moment for us all.

The kids and I went swimming at a local pool. While in the water, some of the boys noticed a white guy with several tattoos. He was in the water with a young boy. My boys got out of the pool to ask me what all the tattoos meant. I looked over at the man, who by now was seated not too far from us. I said, "I don't know. Why don't you go ask him?" The boys trotted over to the man, sat down, and began asking him questions. They returned a bit confused. They explained that the man's tattoos symbolized his pride in white people. He told them that he believed white people are the stronger race. They asked me why he believed that. I replied, "I don't know. Why don't you go ask him?" Off they went.

After a short time, they returned, but were really upset. One announced, "Kori, he hates you. He hates black people. Why does he hate black people?" I shrugged my shoulders and said, "I don't know. What do you think about what he said?" All of the boys expressed the same view: the man was wrong. After all, they explained, he didn't even know me. Why would he hate me?

We returned to the water to play tag. The man and the boy did, too. When they came closer to me, one of my boys swam over to me, followed by the others, and said, "Kori, he's right there." The panic and concern in his voice was clear. The boys surrounded me, creating a wall. I smiled, looked over at the man, and said loud enough for him to hear, "Don't worry he won't do anything to me. They always attack in groups. They never fight one to one. They are cowards." I made eye contact with the man, and then we went our separate ways.

Back in the van, my kids asked, "Kori, what would you have done if he attacked you?" I didn't even blink. I simply said, "One of us would have gotten hurt, and it wouldn't have been me. He would have been fighting for hate. I would have been fighting for my life." The ride back to the Y was much quieter than usual that day.

Note: After so many years dealing with other people's hate, I'm tired. Aren't you? It's 2015. I shouldn't have to worry about being shot by a police officer, being followed in a store, or if I'll lose a family member because they were walking while black. There's no place for this level or kind of hatred in a civil society. But, maybe that's the real problem. Maybe we're not as civil a society as we'd like to believe that we are.

Do Black People Have Tails?

I've often remarked that I wear a sign on my forehead that reads: You can tell me anything. I realized this for the first time when I met my college roommate during freshman year. She was from a small Nebraska town. She was very nice, but very naïve about life outside that little town. Her entire experience with people of other races, especially black people, was from TV and her family and friend's opinions about blacks.

One day, out of the blue, she asked me, "Do black people have tails?" This happened early in the semester. I recall my initial reaction was shock at being asked such a stupid question. How could anyone believe that? I laughed, and said, "No. Why would you think that?" Someone, somewhere, told her that and she wasn't sure if it was true. I told her that she could ask me anything, but to please NOT go around asking other black students questions like that. The "beat-down" that would surely follow would have been terrible! Not everyone would be as open-minded as I was, I told her.

Thankfully, that was the last really offensive question. We got along, though we didn't hang out with each other much. Sometime later in the year, she invited me to a party. I was the only nonwhite, and all they did was drink beer and smoke. I told her she needed to come to a party with me. I can't remember if she ever did.

My life in black and white:

A book of experiences

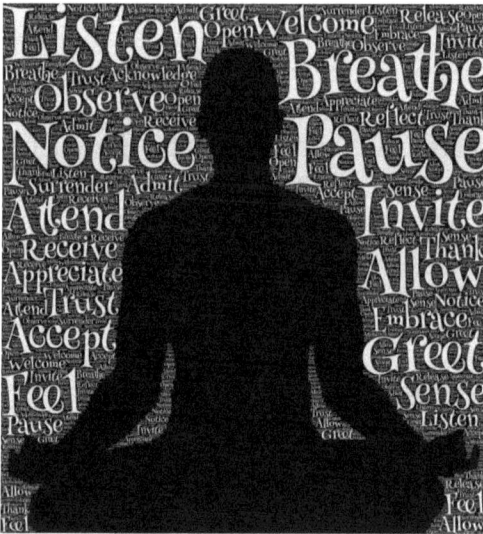

All Grown Up

"I always looked forward to being an adult, because I thought the adult world was, well—adult. That adults weren't cliquey or nasty, that the whole notion of being cool, or in, or popular would cease to be the arbiter of all things social, but I was beginning to realize that the adult world was as nonsensically brutal and socially perilous as the kingdom of childhood."
Peter Cameron, *Someday This Pain Will Be Useful to You*

The Racist

When I saw him, I must confess that I was curious. A devil tattoo clawed at the left side of his neck. White pride symbols screamed from his throat. I was transfixed. He calmly explained what he intended to do. I know what you're thinking. As he reached for my hand, I thought it, too. I wondered. No, I feared. Could this person? Would this person in front of me kill me because I'm not white? I looked down at his outstretched hand. Should I run? His hand was like sandpaper. This was a hard-working man. I looked for the answer in his pale blue, calm eyes. I knew instantly. I had nothing to fear.

I realized, after this originally went to print, that this essay needed more details. Here they are. The above experience happened while I was working in California. At the time, I was a training and development consultant in the Welfare-to-Work field. The man was a recently released, two-time felon required to attend our employment program. We got know each other during the course of my stay. He told me that he was raised by white supremacists. During his first prison term, he did what every prisoner did - segregate. Whites with white, blacks with blacks, and so on. During his second prison stint, he had what he called, a revelation. He made up his mind that he just wanted do his time, get along, get out, and never go back.

He told me that when he got out the second time, he reconnected with his teenage son. During a conversation, he'd asked the young man if he had a girlfriend. The boy hesitated to answer, but eventually said yes. The man asked to see a picture. His son was afraid to show him a picture of his girlfriend because she's black. He assured his son that none of that mattered anymore.

The original essay doesn't quite express the amount of respect I have for this man whose name I've long forgotten. He knew what all the symbols on his body said to me, and to everyone else. And, he was ready to make serious changes. At the time we met, he was in the process of having them removed. We met in the late 90's when removing tattoos wasn't easy and was painful. He considered the pain his penance for having done so many, in his words, stupid things.

He continued through the program and had plans to become a drug and alcohol counselor. I don't know if he accomplished his goal, but I hope that he did.

Oreo Cookie

Have you ever had someone look at you and ask the following questions: What are you? Is that your real hair? If not, you're really missing out! In my adult life, I've been asked these two questions more times than I care to track. As a consultant, I traveled the country training people and speaking at conferences. I finally realized I must be doing something right as a human being. Why? Because I have the ability to make people feel so comfortable with me that they feel free to ask me not only personal questions, but potentially insulting ones.

Many years ago, I was training a group in a small Arizona town. While teaching a section on diversity, one of the trainees had an "ah ha!" moment. She looked at me with a dead-serious expression and said, "So, you're what they call an Oreo cookie, right?" The room got

61

very, very quiet. I looked at her, smiled, and then laughed as I said, "Yes."

On another occasion, I was interviewing a group of African-Americans and Haitians in Ft. Lauderdale, FL. At the time, my hair was long and curly. Out of nowhere, one of the women asked, "Is that your real hair?" At first, I thought this was a strange question. Whose hair would it be? I finally said, "Yes."

I learned early that it's critical for me to take a breath when these things happen. I have to analyze the person's intent. In our efforts to be "PC," I think we've forgotten how important intent actually is. As I explained to my colleagues during one of our many supervisor-training sessions, I know when someone who says black or African-American really means nigger. Intent is everything in race relations. Hell, it's everything in human relations.

Documented Citizen

Have you ever walked down a U.S. street and been asked for "your papers?" It's an enlightening experience. I was reminded of this while talking with one of our employees.

She mentioned that during a trip to Moscow it was common to be asked for one's documents, though she never had the experience. I laughed because in all of my years traveling, the only time I was asked to prove I'm American was in America, or while returning from Tijuana.

Many years ago I was hired to provide employment training in Nogales, AZ. Before going, I spoke with the supervisor to get a feel for the environment. Nogales is a border town. I asked the supervisor if he thought I should bring my passport. He simply said, "As long as you don't look Mexican, you'll be all right." I recall laughing as I said,

"I'll bring it."

I never bothered crossing the border. I didn't even go out at night during the two weeks I was in Nogales. My two previous experiences trying to gain re-entry into the U.S. from Mexico were enough to discourage any exploration of Nogales, Mexico. Being in Nogales, AZ was one of the most uncomfortable experiences I've had as a U.S. citizen.

What people see when they see me is: Mexican, Cuban, Puerto Rican, Hawaiian, Amer-Asian, South American, Middle Eastern — the list goes on and on. I'm a blender and I'm an American citizen.

Marry White or Black?

During my first marriage, I began traveling more for my job. I was visiting an employment training site in Ft. Lauderdale, FL. The class was comprised of African-Americans and Haitians. I was visiting the site to take pictures of participants, and to learn more about their training program. After about an hour, the group felt comfortable with me. How did I know?

A member of the group asked, "Did you marry a white guy or a black guy?"

Before I continue, let me explain an interesting phenomena in my life, thus far. It seems that black people almost always know that I'm interracial, or in their view, black. American Caucasians, people of Hispanic origin, Middle-Eastern people, some Europeans, and some Asians, don't know, when looking at me, what my race is actually.

There's usually a lot of stammering and stuttering when they try to figure it out, especially if they're American Caucasians.

So, when the participant asked this question, (a question I've only received from black people), I smiled, chuckled a bit, and said, "Are those my only choices?" Then I posed a challenge: I'll show you a picture of my husband. If you can guess his background, then I'll give you all the money in my wallet. You each get one guess.

After each trainee had an opportunity to study his picture and guess incorrectly, I gave them the answer.

"My husband is Arab; Palestinian, to be exact. He grew up in the UAE." The group was stunned. I was happy to keep my money that day.

No, I'm Not the Nanny

When our third baby unexpectedly died, my second husband, who had just arrived in his hotel in Calgary, CN, hopped a return flight to be with me. After dealing with the medical side and making a few arrangements, we packed our other two children into our truck and began a four day trek north to Calgary.

We spent three weeks in Calgary during our initial trip and another three on a return visit. My husband and I have always traveled well together, and our preference is to be together during business trips, whenever possible.

We ended up really liking Calgary. It has a diversity that is truly lacking where we are living. Because of that diversity, our children were able to play with people from many parts of the world at the various playgrounds the children and I visited, daily. It was common to hear a variety of languages spoken. Our children quickly adapted to their surroundings.

Every day, I would take the children to one or two playgrounds. We enjoy finding new ones and when we find a few favorites, we go back again, and again. Playgrounds have personalities. There's the "I have money or like to pretend I do" playground, the neighborhood playground, the "we might have money, but we don't boast about it playground" and the "in the city trying to pretend it's the country" state-park playground. The neighborhood playground personality simply depends on the area -- could be rich, could be poor. That will dictate the behavior of both parent and child on the playground. The state-park playground usually has a hodgepodge of "not so well off" to "upper middle class," and is always an interesting mix.

One day, while visiting one of our favorite in-the-city state parks, a woman asked me an odd question. She asked if I was the nanny. I laughed, said "no," and asked "why?" She replied that I seemed to be so much nicer to my children, playing with them, and giving them direction as needed, that she thought I might be a nanny.

"A good nanny is so difficult to find," she said. We had some discussion about why my children look white. There was a bit of backpedalling on her part because she really didn't mean to offend me. Right.

I'd like to say this was my only experience being regarded as "the nanny" for our two children, but it wasn't. I was truly astounded at the number of nannies I encountered. And, not one of them was white. Why is that?

And, why do white women presume that it's okay to ask if the children are mine? One woman actually said of my daughter, "she doesn't look like you." Well, it's a good thing DNA testing exists, huh?

The sad thing about these interactions is that the women asking never even realize just how offensive their questions are. They never seem to think, "Maybe I should ask this a different way," or "Maybe it really isn't any of my business," or "Maybe I should simply compliment the child's nice manners." No, instead, I must be the nanny because my children apparently don't look like me; therefore, it's okay to be intrusive and insulting.

I've received a bit of feedback since writing this essay. Some readers feel that I'm ranting. You're right, I am, and with good reason. There's nothing more annoying than having someone question my relationship to my children. My husband is never asked if our children are his. The overall lesson here is one I teach my children:

Think before you speak. You have two ears and one mouth for a reason.

Out with the Old

Today is March 31, 2007. I just had to write that down to remind myself. You see, in 2007 I expect that when I pay to eat breakfast somewhere, I'll be able to enjoy my meal. I expect that I won't have to overhear conversations about mulattos and how awful it would be if my "son or daughter married outside of 'The Race'." I expect that people in 2007 would have more consideration, more tact, and more respect for those around them, but this expectation has been proved wrong time and time, again. This is truly sad when you realize we are just entering the fourth month of a new year.

The three older white women who were having this conversation seemed completely oblivious to my presence. I was seated right next to their table. One of them talked about some man marrying some younger woman and that they would probably not have children, so it didn't matter. The next thing I know, this woman is talking about Dancing with The Stars and the mulatto on the show. I know very little about the show. Another woman mentioned how attractive "those" people can be. The first woman hesitated to agree, but eventually conceded, but admitted she would never want one in her family. The third woman said, "You hate to have to disown your own family members..." That hung in the air as the others simply nodded in agreement. The second woman explained how there are more of "them" than white people in the world. This realization seemed to really distress the other two.

When I initially overheard the word "mulatto" come out of the first woman's mouth, the hair on the back of my neck stood up. At one point, I made eye contact with the woman who made the "more of them comment," but there was no recognition by her that what they were discussing was being overheard and offensive. They simply carried on lamenting the fact that their white race isn't as pure as it once was. Pure. One of them actually used that word.

I struggled with whether I should say anything to them. What would I say? What would it have accomplished? They had to be in their late 60s or early 70s. All I can hope is that they die soon and that their poisonous words don't fall on impressionable ears. I would like to believe this was an isolated incident, but I know it wasn't. Just this past week, a young black teenager received voicemail threats from a white teenager. The "n" word was thrown about and there was the threat of hanging the young black teenager at a local park.

Today is Jan. 15, 2009, and we are poised to inaugurate the first interracial president of the United States. I wonder what those ladies are saying about that?

This essay was originally published in *Fine Lines Literary Journal*, Summer 2009 edition.

Note: Each time I read this piece, I choke back the bile at the back of my throat. These women disgusted me in a way very few others have ever been able to accomplish. The amount of entitlement these women possessed was astounding. It must be interesting to go through one's entire life believing that because you are white, you can say and do whatever you like, whenever you like, without regard for those around you. Wow. Just, wow.

My life in black and white:

A book of experiences

A 40 Year Old's Perspective

"Often the adult book is not for you, not yet, or will only be for you when you're ready. But sometimes you will read it anyway, and you will take from it whatever you can. Then, perhaps, you will come back to it when you're older, and you will find the book has changed because you have changed as well, and the book is wiser, or more foolish, because you are wiser or more foolish than you were as a child."

Neil Gaiman

I Can't See White People

I can't see white people. Seriously. You know how some white people say, "All black people look alike?" Well, I discovered that sometimes, I just can't see white people. It might be that some of them are simply too light. Their camouflage is really that good. For instance, one day, I was out and about, doing errands or something, and my husband (who is white, by the way) said, "Watch out!" I was completely startled, and just missed some white guy, blending in, crossing the street! "Where the &*^%$ did he come from?" I said to my husband, all exasperated.

I thought, maybe this is a fluke or something. I didn't grow up not being able to see white people. Half my family is white. Then, one morning it happened again! I was driving up a hill, close to our house, when out of nowhere this white woman popped up. (Actually, I noticed her little grey/brown dog on a leash first. Really, it was the leash. The dog is small and just as difficult to see. Luckily, it was moving.) That's what made my mind go, "Huh, what's that dog doin' out here on a leash by itself?" And, then I saw her. Dammit if she didn't just blend right into the pavement with her light hair, pale skin, white shorts, and gray sweatshirt. Gravel. That's all I saw. Oh, and the dog with the leash. Why can't she wear something, anything, that glows, or maybe even flashes?

It's very disturbing when you realize you can't see a certain group of people. Once or twice, and you can convince yourself your mind is simply playing tricks on you. After repeated episodes, it becomes unsettling. Is this the beginning of becoming "color blind?" It starts with the pale-skinned white people, then slowly moves to the darker-skinned people? No! That can't be right.

I never appreciated the term "color-blind," until now. Surely this is what people mean when they use the term. After all, the world would be a more peaceful place if we couldn't actually see color. Oh wait, that's not what I mean. That would be like living the movie "Pleasantville" twenty-four-seven. That would suck.

Years ago, I was asked, "If you could be any color in the world, what color would you be?" It was for a job interview. I applied to work as a Resident Assistant in a dorm during college. I appeared thoughtful before responding, "I'd be a sort of clear, waxy color." Of course, the interviewers followed-up with "Why?" The answer was simple: I wanted people to see me for who I am and not for the color of my skin. Color-blind.

Now, I'm 40+ years old and realize just how awful that world would be. Being "color blind" isn't what I want. Can you imagine walking down a street, and every person you see is sort of waxy? They'd be like outlines or sketches. Ridiculous. I want to see every color! I want to bask in the glow of my light-skinned, light-haired baby girl's smile. When that shadow shows in the creases of my son's dimples, I want to see it. My soul fills with warmth every time I see my pale-skinned, Northern European husband's bright blue eyes twinkle -- just like his father's did -- when he's trying to be sneaky. I don't want a color-blind life.

Note: I hesitated to include this essay. My intent is that you read it with a light heart and that you see the humor, irony, and overall message it contains. This essay started with a few sentences that made me laugh. Over the course of a year, I revised it several times. I asked people to read it and to give me feedback. This is the result. I still see the woman I mentioned. And, I still wish she'd wear some sort of reflective clothing, but that really doesn't have anything to do with the color of her skin. It's simply a safety issue. - KDM

Our Lawn Burned

The night our lawn burned, a neighbor rang our doorbell. I remember thinking, "What would have happened if they hadn't?" Later, I thought, "Maybe these white people, don't want us here." My parents sent us back to bed.

I awoke the next morning, dressed for school, walked outside, and saw it for the first time. A dark, half moon invaded the late-to-get green zoysia grass. The little hairs on my neck stood at attention. I shivered, though it was a warm day. I couldn't be late for school, but I also couldn't walk away. Why would someone do this? I stepped on it. A little "puff" of ash lifted around my foot.

My parents didn't seem rattled by it. Maybe they were used to this sort of thing. We didn't talk about it much. It was simply -- there. In fact, it was there for a long time. It was laughing at us.

Every morning I walked by our burned lawn. I stopped. I stared. At first, I looked around to see if someone was watching. After a while, it didn't matter anymore. I was afraid, but more than that, I was angry. I was 8-years-old.

I don't know if my parents called the police. I don't remember how the fire went out. All I remember, is that one day our nice, new home, and late-to-get-green zoysia grass, was perfect. The next day it was scarred.

There were other incidents, I'm sure, but none as dramatic as that welcome. I've never discussed it with my parents or older brother. What would be the point?

Over the years, many people, mostly white, asked, "Do you think things are better, now?" I'm never sure why they're asking me. Is it because I'm interracial? Does that somehow make them more comfortable? They certainly aren't asking because they see me as white. They see me as different, and they ask this question that they can't ask other white people. What would another white person say? "Why , yes, I think things are just swell!" or "No, there's too many of them! They're going to outnumber us by 2040!" What are these white people looking for when they ask me this question? What do they expect me to say?

I have 40+ years of experience not being 100% white. Forty plus years of not fitting into a little bubble on a sheet of paper, or in someone's mind. And, I've spent at least half of that time answering that one question.

The night our lawn burned, I would have liked to have asked at least one white person, "Why?"

My life in black and white:

A book of experiences

Final Thoughts

"Have patience with everything
that remains unsolved in your
heart.
...live in the question."
Rainer Maria Rilke, *Letters to a
Young Poet*

That's it. That's all I have to say on the subject of race in America. Since 2011, I've talked publicly about my book once. I've been interviewed via the internet two or three times, and there's one audio interview out there.

The first essay I published on the subject of being interracial is, *Zebras, Half-breeds and Oreo Cookies*. This essay was originally written while I attended college. I sent it to *Fine Lines Literary Journal* many years later as a response to an article I'd read. The author of that article was having an identity crisis of sorts.

These essays span more than 30 years of experiences being interracial in America. My hope is that young people find them helpful. I was surprised to learn that most of my readers are adults looking for answers and insights into the question of being interracial/biracial in America.

Writing this book of essays

served three purposes for me: First, I learned how to self-publish a book. Second, I gave my children something they could read later, so that they'd understand what my life as an interracial person has been like. And, third, I let the new generation of biracial kids know that they're not alone in their experiences. What I didn't expect was the feedback from adult readers, most of which has been positive and constructive.

During the one book talk I gave at our local library, someone asked if I was treated differently, i.e., better during my travels overseas. Yes, I was. I don't have an explanation for that. It's simply true. It's also sad and frustrating. But, that wasn't my reason, and still isn't my reason, for wanting to travel or live overseas. I love people, places, variety, diversity — and food, I can't neglect to mention the food. Traveling or living abroad expands my world view. That's one of the things I want my children to experience. My perspective here can best be summed up by a quote from *Auntie Mame*: Life is a banquet and most poor suckers are starving to death! Live! Live! Live!

I've also been asked if my brother's experience was the same as mine. I don't know. Not every interracial/bi-racial person has the same experience even in the same family. And, he and I don't talk about it much. I know some of his experiences, but they're his to share, not mine.

Several times since 2011, I've been asked to participate in interviews or surveys about being interracial/biracial, but I've declined to do so. The reason is simple; I don't like dwelling in dark places. While I believe the experiences I'm sharing are important, I don't enjoy spending my time rehashing them, or revisiting how I felt at the time they happened. It's enough for me to have it on paper. These days, I spend my writing time focused on more upbeat things. Writing essays has, and always will be, a way for me to express my feelings and experiences, but once it's on paper, it's time for me to move forward. My view is best summed up in a quote by Walt Disney: Keep moving forward.

Some people wanted to know why I choose to describe myself as interracial instead of biracial. Years ago, biracial was still a new term and I didn't care for it. Something about it seemed limiting. I chose interracial because, in my mind, it's more inclusive of who I am racially and ethnically. My overall preference is human.

I've also been asked if my husband and I gave any thought to how we'd be treated as a couple or how our children might be treated. We did, and we still do. As I pointed out to each of those people, you can't control who you love. You can certainly limit your dating pool, if you want, but we chose not to do that. That choice meant that we had to talk about the subject of race. For the record, we've never been treated badly by anyone during any of our travels. Not when we were together, at any rate. There have been a few incidents that happened when I was alone, as described in some of the essays, and there was a police encounter that quickly changed direction when the officer saw my husband is white, but that's really all. When we travel in the US, we take into consideration where we're going or what states we're traveling through. We'd be foolish not to. It's better to be prepared than to be surprised.

People also wanted to know what we say to our children about their race. The short answer is that they're human, like everyone else. The longer answer involves details about our racial/ethnic breakdown and that most people will see them as white. We also discuss what that might mean for them as they grow older. We don't spend a lot of time talking about racial issues because of their ages right now. When they have questions, we answer them. And, they're not involved in our discussions about travel routes.

That about raps it up, I think. If you or others have more questions, you can visit www.koridmiller.com. If your question isn't answered there, then feel free to send me an email.

Keep moving forward!
Kori

My life in black and white:

A book of experiences

Thank you to all who read the first edition of *My Life in Black and White: A book of experiences*. Sharing your stories with me is appreciated.

Thank you, Jenn Carter, for designing the cover. I still love it.

Thank you to my editor, Larry Miller, for your continued support and great, on-point feedback.

Thank you to the special editors of *Fine Lines Literary Journal* for your willingness to include some of my essays in the journal, even when you knew others might be offended. Life is about taking chances. Thanks for taking the chance on me.

Please consider leaving a review on Amazon.com. Thank you!

Kori Miller is the co-founder and CEO of MEEI (Miller-Ericksen Enterprises, Inc.) MEEI was established in 2003 and operates The Tea Trove in Nebraska. The company specializes in hand-blended teas, tisanes, and lemonades. She is a partner in Neskcire Systems, Inc.: a controls system and robotics development company founded in 2009. Ms. Miller is an author, essayist, and storyteller. Her first book titled, *My*

Life in Black and White: A book of experiences was published in 2011. Her second book titled, *Deadly Sins: A Dezeray Jackson Mini-Series* was published February 2014. Her first children's book, titled, *Dante,* was published December 2014. She's published essays and short fiction in *Fine Lines Literary Journal* since 2007, is the author of *The Road Warrior's Guide to Plugging In* available at *Cozy Couples Magazine* online, and her flash fiction piece titled, *Found*, won first place in a *Flash-Fiction World* contest in 2013. She is the founder and host of Back Porch Writer: The show for writers, about writers, and writing on Blog Talk Radio. Away from work, Ms. Miller spends time with her family, and studies Hapkido.

Look for these titles in 2015:

Adult Titles:
Deadly Sins II
*Hush: A Dezeray Jackson
Novel*

Children's Titles:
Dante in the Woods
Dante and the Cold, Dark Night
Splash!

Middle Grade Titles:
*The Coyote Wars: Radalov's
Vengeance*

Look for these titles in 2016:

Adult Titles:
North Downing:
A Dezeray Jackson Novel

Middle Grade Titles:
The Compass Wars

My life in black and white:

A book of experiences

Deadly Sins is written in a flash fiction style. These quotes sum up each story, and my approach quite well.

Some stories are true that never happened. – Elie Wiesel

Fiction is about stuff that's screwed up. – Nancy Kress

All the information you need, can be given in dialogue. – Elmore Leonard

Enjoy the snippet! Buy the book. It's available on Amazon.com.

Read Kori's first book in the Dezeray Jackson Mini-Series!

Deadly Sins: A Dezeray Jackson Mini-Series

Three murders. Two stolen artifacts. Three states. One private investigator. Deadly sins led them to commit the crimes, but which ones? Read the stories. You decide.

Private investigator Dezeray Jackson hates Florida; she hated it 24 hours after she arrived 5 years ago. Not for any particular reason, really, just a whole lot of little ones — bugs, alligators, snakes, and rude, obnoxious people. Dez thinks a break is in order, then she gets the Millicent James case. All she has to do is follow Millicent's gamer grandson for a month, which could be as exciting as waiting for water to boil, Dez thinks. But a boring, routine assignment suddenly takes some interesting twists when a much-anticipated pre-release game disappears. It's a hot commodity that could make somebody millions of dollars. But who?

After two years in the Big Apple, Dez is fed up with cheating spouses and embezzling employees. Convinced that she needs a change, Dez tells her boss that she's ready to move on. He gives her a farewell gift — one last case, involving a missing artifact. Dez and her partner hit the streets, and soon learn that the missing artifact is something more. To recover it, Dez will enter a world that few know about. Dez thought she'd seen it all ... she hadn't.

When Dez left New York, she didn't think she"d end up back in Omaha, NE, her home town. But here she is three months later. After stints in Florida and the Big Apple, Omaha was an unexpected, but welcome change. But the grass isn't always greener on the other side. One evening, after hearing Dez speak to her female self-defense class, a student is killed in a hit-and-run. Dez gets the case, which leads to an unpleasant stroll down memory lane, with a character she'd rather forget, and involvement with some deadly corporate shenanigans.

Eccentric Mayville Toussaint hires Dez to find two men who stole a box from her. Toussaint's instructions are simple — find the thieves, recover the box, and return it unopened. A dangerous game of cat and mouse, double-dealing and lying place Dez in harm's way. Dez recovers the box — case closed. But when returning the treasured item, Dez learns that Toussaint has been playing her own game of cat and mouse ... with Dez. Toussaint clearly is not who she seems. But who is she?

My life in black and white:

A book of experiences

www.ingramcontent.com/pod-product-compliance
Lightning Source LLC
Chambersburg PA
CBHW071817020426
42331CB00007B/1512